COFFEE ART
MASTERCLASS

COFFEE ART
MASTERCLASS

50 incredible coffee designs
for the home barista

Dhan
Tamang

First published in Great Britain in 2024 by Cassell,
an imprint of Octopus Publishing Group Ltd,
Carmelite House,
50 Victoria Embankment,
London EC4Y 0DZ
www.octopusbooks.co.uk

An Hachette UK Company
www.hachette.co.uk

Distributed in the US by Hachette Book Group,
1290 Avenue of the Americas, 4th and 5th Floors,
New York, NY 10104

Distributed in Canada by Canadian Manda Group,
664 Annette St., Toronto, Ontario, Canada M6S 2C8

ISBN 978-1-78840-464-8

A CIP catalogue record for this book is available from the British Library.

Printed and bound in China.

1 3 5 7 9 10 8 6 4 2

MIX
Paper | Supporting
responsible forestry
FSC
www.fsc.org
FSC® C008047

Publisher: Trevor Davies
Art Director: Yasia Williams
Senior Editor: Leanne Bryan
Editorial Assistant: Stephanie Selcuk-Frank
Copy Editor: Caroline West
Photographers: Jason Ingram and Chris Terry
Designer: Claire Huntley
Assistant Production Manager: Lisa Pinnell

Additional text by Stephanie Selcuk-Frank, Trevor Davies and Abi Waters.

With thanks to Sanremo for the use of their UK showroom for photoshoots
and to the London School of Coffee.

Picture Credits

Photography by Jason Ingram: 7–16, 30, 32, 40, 42, 54, 58, 98, 122.
All other coffee photography by Chris Terry.

Additional images: 51a Peter van Evert; 54a, 60a, 63 Public domain
via Wikimedia Commons; 56a Martin Shields/Alamy Stock Photo © Salvador Dali, Fundacio
Gala-Salvador Dali, DACS 2024; 58 The National Museum, Norway,
Object NG.M 00939; 64 Christie's Images/Bridgeman Images © ADAGP,
Paris and DACS, London 2024.

CONTENTS

INTRODUCTION

Since I wrote my first book six years ago, latte art has evolved to include not only iconic designs like hearts, tulips and rosettas, but also more complex and sophisticated images that use different techniques, colours, patterns and shading to create visually spectacular effects. So, unlock your creativity and learn the art and craft of the barista and coffee artist.

WHAT EQUIPMENT WILL I NEED?

You will need very little equipment to create coffee art, but here is a rundown of the basics:

• **A coffee machine** - to make the espresso.

• **A milk frother** - these can be as basic or as expensive as you can afford and are used to steam and froth the milk for making lattes, cappuccinos and dry foam (a thick cappuccino foam). You may have a full coffee machine with a steaming wand to meet all your needs, but you can achieve the same results with a basic milk frother.

• **A pouring jug** - to pour the steamed and frothed milk into your espresso. A narrow spout will help ensure a steady flow of milk when pouring the more intricate designs. Look for jugs with a well-designed, comfortable handle too, as this will allow you to pour smoothly, without straining your hand or wrist.

• **Coffee cups in different sizes** - from espresso cups (60ml/2fl oz) to a large cappuccino cup (300ml/ 10fl oz), depending on how big you like your coffee. Most designs work better in a larger cup, as they provide more room for manoeuvre when free pouring and make fiddly movements less challenging.

• **A range of etching tools** - you can use anything to etch, such as the handle of a teaspoon or a bradawl (woodworking tool). Use a cocktail stick or skewer for finer details. You may also need a small spatula.

• **A damp cloth** - for wiping the etching tool clean between etches.

• **Liquid food colouring** - to colour milk foam. Pour into an expresso cup, using more for deeper shades.

• **Thick card and a scalpel** - most designs use free pouring, but you will need to make a stencil for some.

STEAMING AND FROTHING MILK

You will need to steam and froth milk to pour into an espresso to create the base or crema (see page 8). The texture of the foam should be velvety. The amount of milk foam you need depends on the size of cup you are using. For a 300ml (10fl oz) cup, you will need 235ml (8½fl oz) of cold milk. The milk should be frothed and steamed to about 60°C (140°F).

WHAT TYPE OF MILK WORKS BEST?

Whole milk is the preferred choice for many baristas when creating coffee art. The higher fat content contributes to a richer and creamier texture, which helps stabilize the foam when crafting designs. Plant-based alternatives such as soya, almond, hazelnut and oat milk can be used, but their composition and texture is not as stable as dairy milk when frothed, meaning more intricate designs may need further practice.

WHAT IS A CREMA?

The 'crema' is the velvety, caramel-coloured foam that naturally forms on top as the coffee is poured. This creamier texture differs to the liquid espresso below, acting as a natural foundation for baristas to create defined lines and shapes. Simply pouring milk into a coffee without following the basic steps on the following page will destroy the crema and leave you with no pattern on top of your coffee, so take care!

CREATING THE BASE

Creating the base, or crema, is the first step in coffee art design. This combination of espresso and steamed/frothed milk forms a special 'canvas' onto which baristas can pour milk, producing intricate patterns and designs.

Pour an espresso into any size of cup (here we used a 300ml/10fl oz cup). Position the cup so the handle is facing away from you and then tilt the cup by 45 degrees.

Pour the steamed milk into the middle of the coffee from a height of about 8cm (3 inches). The milk will go into the espresso, but the crema will stay on the top to create a layer of soft froth.

Pour in a consistent stream, zigzagging the flow of milk across the cup, left to right and back again, as if you are drawing smiles across the cup as it fills up. This will maintain the crema.

As you pour, lower the jug closer to the cup until it is two-thirds full (or as required by the recipe). Create your design as instructed.

MAKING A QUENELLE

To make a quenelle of foam, you will need a teaspoon and dessert spoon. Scrape the milk foam from one spoon to the other until you have a thick and stiff foam. Don't be afraid of overworking the foam because this will create a better and more malleable consistency, ideal for creating 3D designs.

GOOD TECHNIQUE

1. Move your wrist rather than your arm to keep the pouring and etching steady. You can also support the forearm of your pouring hand with the other hand.

2. Take a deep breath before you start and slowly let it out as you pour - this will help you stay steady and focused. I also stand with a wide and firm stance, so I don't wobble while pouring - this has been nicknamed the 'Dhan Tamang Stand'.

3. Bang the cup on the work surface to get rid of any bubbles on the milk surface. This also levels out the foam if making 3D designs.

4. Ensure the milk always flows into the hole created by the pouring - known as 'following the white'.

5. After steaming and frothing the milk, pour a little of the milk foam into a small espresso cup to be used in the designs later.

6. The instructions are written from the perspective of a right-handed person, so bear this in mind if you are left-handed. The cup is also treated like a clock face, with the handle at 3 o'clock. Use the finished photograph for guidance when positioning the elements of a design and work in a way that feels comfortable for you.

7. To make the foam for 3D designs, heat the milk to 64–65°C (147–149°F), then froth it until doubled in size. This stiffened, aerated foam is called dry foam and should be kept in a separate jug. Next, use the quenelle technique (see opposite) to thicken and stiffen the foam enough to make shapes.

BASIC DESIGNS

HEART

The heart is the easiest coffee art design and one of the first that baristas are taught. You may be familiar with this classic design already, as it is frequently seen in coffee shops around the world!

1 Create the base in a coffee cup (see page 8).

2 Once the cup is two-thirds full, drop the jug closer to the cup and pour into the side closest to you – this will begin to create the heart shape, as a white circle will start forming on the surface and get larger as you pour.

Continue pouring until you have created a large white circle of foam.

3

4 Once the cup is almost full and you have created a large white circle of foam, bring the stream upwards and draw a line of milk through the middle of the circle to create the heart shape.

TULIP

Once you've mastered pouring a heart you can develop this into a tulip. Alone the tulip is a simple, yet pretty design, but it can also be used as the basis for the more complex patterns featured later on.

Create the base in a coffee cup (see page 8). When the cup is around two-thirds full, stop pouring.

Keeping the cup at an angle, pour foam into the centre to create a small milk circle, then stop, drawing up slightly at the end to create a kind of heart shape.

Create another slightly smaller circle of milk above the first one, again bringing the jug up at the end to create the heart shape.

Pour a third, smaller circle of milk above the second, but this time finish by lifting the jug and running the milk through the middle of all three circles to create your tulip.

ROSETTA

The rosetta is a latte art design resembling a delicate, swirling leaf or floral pattern. This is more advanced than the heart design and, like the tulip, it is used in many of the other designs throughout the book.

1 Create the base in a coffee cup (see page 8).

2 Once the cup is two-thirds full, drop the jug closer to the cup and continue pouring to form a white circle on the surface. This will be the base of your rosetta. Now start wiggling the jug left to right as you pour.

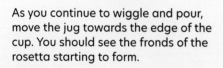

As you continue to wiggle and pour, move the jug towards the edge of the cup. You should see the fronds of the rosetta starting to form.

3

4 When you near the edge of the cup, lift the jug to about 3cm (1 inch) away from the surface and finish with a line of milk through the middle of the design – this will create a strong-looking leaf.

ADVANCED DESIGNS
SLOSETTA

This is effectively a very slowly – or lazily – poured rosetta. You may think that a slosetta looks like a novice trying to pour a rosetta, but it does take a sure and steady hand to make a slosetta look impressive.

1 Create the base in a coffee cup (see page 8), pouring until the cup is half-full.

2 Starting at the top of the cup, pour a rosetta (see opposite), but now instead of wiggling the jug, draw slow loops from left to right, narrowing as you move down the cup.

When you reach the bottom of the cup, pause briefly to create a circle at the top of the slosetta.

3

4 Pour a line through the centre of the circle and then all the way through the design to finish.

TOP TIP

To achieve thicker lines than the normal rosetta, be sure to keep your hand steady and the pattern slow.

DOUBLE HEART

The secret of this beautifully simple pattern is to create a heart within a heart. This is done by pouring two hearts, one on top of the other. As you pour, the second heart pushes the outline of the first to the edge of the cup, resulting in concentric hearts.

1 Create the base in a coffee cup (see page 8).

2 Pour a heart (see page 10), but rather than pouring a line all the way through the circle to finish, stop halfway - so that the heart is not yet fully formed.

3 Now pour another circle, just below the first one.

4 Pour and move to the middle of the cup, pausing to add more milk to the centre to enlarge the circle. The second circle will expand into the first one as you pour, creating a double layered circle. Raise the jug from the surface and then pour a line through the centre of both circles to create the double heart design.

WINGED TULIP

This abstract design combines rosettas with a tulip to create a flower with extended petal-like wings on either side. This is a more challenging design, but don't be disheartened. With time and practice, you'll soon be able to achieve the desired symmetry and shape.

1 Create the base in a coffee cup (see page 8) and pour until the cup is half-full.

2 To create the wings, pour a rosetta (see page 12), starting in the centre of the cup and moving to the right. Wiggle the jug and push the rosetta to the left as you pour, then finish about halfway across the cup by pouring through the centre of the rosetta.

3 Next, pour a tulip (see page 11), starting in the centre of the cup, just underneath the rosetta. Add as many layers to the tulip as you like (or can fit in). As you pour, you will push the tulip into the rosetta, so the rosetta spreads out around the tulip to form the extended wings.

4 Raise the jug and pour through the centre of the tulip to finish.

MULTI-LAYERED TULIP

This builds upon the simple tulip design by adding multiple layers of milk to give the appearance of a blooming flower. The key to achieving the extra layers is to start the tulip sooner in the pouring process, so don't fill the cup too full before beginning your design.

Create the base in a coffee cup (see page 8), but stop pouring when the cup is one-third full.

Keeping the cup at an angle, pour your first circle in the centre of the cup to create the basic tulip design (see page 11).

Start the second circle slightly below the first, moving the stream of milk up as you pour to push the circle higher in the cup.

Continue to pour layers beneath one another until you reach the bottom side of the cup, making them smaller each time.

Finish by raising the jug and drawing a line through the middle of all the circles to create a multi-layered tulip.

FOR
NATURE LOVERS

SUN AND MOON

This fun design can be created swiftly once mastered, then embellished as much as you like with more comets, planets and cosmic ephemera, and even the Solar System – although you might need a bigger cup for this.

Prepare an espresso cup of orange milk foam and a second cup with a small amount of black food colouring, then set these to one side. Create the base in a large coffee cup (see page 8), pouring until the cup is two-thirds full.

2 To form the moon, pour a winged tulip with two layers (see page 15), starting by the handle 2.5cm (1 inch) away from the edge of the cup.

3 To begin the sun, pour a circle of milk above the tulip 2.5cm (1 inch) away from the edge of the cup. Using a tablespoon, gently dollop a circle of orange milk foam over the white circle, to give the sun some colour.

4 Use a fine-tipped tool to draw the moon's eye and eyelashes with the black food colouring. For the nose, add a small circle of white milk foam, left over in the jug. Add a smile, or any expression you wish.

5 Turning back to the sun, equip yourself with a clean etching tool. Now drag the orange milk foam from the edge of the circle outwards and slightly to the right. This will create curvy lines coming out from the sun, which are the sun's rays.

Use a clean fine-tipped tool and the black food colouring to paint on the sun's face.

Use a teaspoon handle to drop five circles of evenly spaced white milk, starting at the 10 o'clock position and ending at 1 o'clock. Drop four circles of evenly spaced white milk from the 7 o'clock position to the 4 o'clock position (these will be stars).

To give some of the stars a little sparkle, drag the milk from the middle of the circles outwards, extending beyond the outline.

For a final touch, create a shooting star. Add some extra milk to the star on the right at the top, then drag the milk outwards to create a tail. To smudge the tail, use a fine-tipped tool to pull the milk diagonally up and down.

DOVE

This is a serene and elegant design that combines three delicate rosettas to create the dove's body, wings and tail.

1 Prepare an espresso cup of orange milk foam and set this to one side. Create the base in a large coffee cup (see page 8), pouring until the cup is two-thirds full.

2 Pour a rosetta (see page 12) with the cup tilted away from you, starting from the middle of the cup and ending towards the handle. Pour a second rosetta, starting from the middle and ending on the opposite side. These will be the wings of the dove.

To create the dove's tail, pour a rosetta from the 5 o'clock to the 7 o'clock position. As you near the end of the rosetta, lift the jug higher and keep pouring to connect the tail to the body. Repeat this movement on the other side of the rosetta.

3

4 Once the wings and tail are formed, use a cocktail stick or other etching tool to add more detail to the dove's tail. Drag the cocktail stick gently upwards through the milk to create feathers within the tail.

Dollop a small circle of milk foam above the middle of the wings to form the head. Then drag this dot outwards slightly to the left to form the beak. If the milk foam has deflated slightly, you may need to colour in the dove's body with extra milk.

5

6

Paint the dove's feet and beak with the orange milk foam to finish the design.

SWAN

With practice, an ugly duckling can be transformed into a majestic swan. Whether floating elegantly along a river or in countryside lakes and ponds, this gliding swan combines tulips and rosettas to form an alluring design.

Create the base in a small coffee cup (see page 8), pouring until two-thirds full. Pour a four-layered tulip (see page 11), starting just below the 3 o'clock position, 2.5cm (1 inch) away from the side, and finishing at 2 o'clock.

Pour a rosetta (see page 12) next to the tulip in one motion, starting from the middle of the cup and dragging outwards to the 12 o'clock position.

Starting from the middle of the cup again, pour a second rosetta next to the first one.

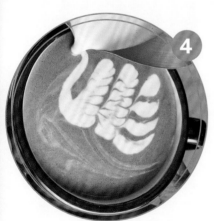

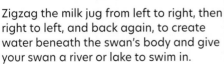

Tilting the cup slightly, pour a thin stream of milk upwards, curving to create the swan's body and neck. Pause momentarily at the top of the neck and then drag the jug downwards slightly to form a heart. This will be the swan's head.

Zigzag the milk jug from left to right, then right to left, and back again, to create water beneath the swan's body and give your swan a river or lake to swim in.

KINGFISHER

Dive straight into this dashing design, where vibrant blue hearts combine with a winged tulip to create an iridescent kingfisher!

Prepare an espresso cup of blue milk foam and set this to one side. Create a smooth and solid base in a large coffee cup (see page 8), pouring until the cup is two-thirds full. Once the base layer is in place, pour a winged tulip with two layers (see page 15).

2 Dollop three small circles of blue milk foam to create the kingfisher's body. The first dot should be positioned at the 12 o'clock position, 2.5cm (1 inch) away from the edge of the cup. The second dot should be just below the first and the final dot below the second, in the centre of the coffee.

Use a cocktail stick or other etching tool to drag the foam from the edge of the cup inwards, to add some definition to the outer wings.

3

4 With a clean etching tool, scoop up some milk left over from the jug and add white dots around the outer wings. Gently drag each dot towards the inner tulip, to make the dots look like splashes.

Holding the etching tool tightly, pull downwards through the three blue dots to turn the circles into heart shapes.

5

6 With the last of the blue milk foam, draw two curved lines either side of the middle of the kingfisher's body, to form the protruding wings.

SEAHORSE

Take an intriguing dip into the world of seahorses and unlock the magic of these elegant, yet extraordinary marine beings, all on the surface of your morning coffee.

1. Create the base in a large coffee cup (see page 8), pouring until the cup is half full.

2. Pour a small, multi-layered tulip (see pages 16–17), starting 2.5cm (1 inch) away from the edge of the cup at the 3 o'clock position. This will form the dorsal fin of the seahorse.

To shape the seahorse's body, first pour a rosetta (see page 12), starting from the middle of the cup and pouring diagonally right and down. The rosetta should finish at around 5 o'clock.

3

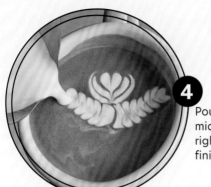

4

Pour a second rosetta, starting from the middle of the cup and pouring diagonally right and upwards. This rosetta should finish at around 1 o'clock.

5

To create the bubbles, free pour a rosetta towards the side of the cup - starting around the 8 o'clock position and pouring vertically upwards until you reach 10 o'clock. Outline the top of the seahorse's body by pouring carefully in a downwards motion along the front (tummy) area of the second rosetta, raising the jug upwards to create a fine stream of milk. Curve the seahorse's tail at the end of the first rosetta by free pouring a spiral of milk.

To shape the seahorse's head, pour a small spiral on top of the second rosetta. Continue pouring, dragging outwards to the left. Now pause for a moment before forming a smaller circle to create the seahorse's snout.

6

CHERRY BLOSSOM

Despite the name, this lovely design uses crushed dried rose petals to create the illusion of cherry blossom. Not only does this give a beautiful finish to the design, but it also adds a lovely taste to the coffee. Try a rich blend of coffee to match the rose flavour, or even try it with hot chocolate.

Prepare two espresso cups of milk foam in black and pink, and set these to one side. Create the base in a small coffee cup (see page 8), pouring until the cup is two-thirds full.

Pour milk into the centre of the coffee cup to create a circle.

Use an etching tool to outline the tree trunk with the black milk foam, moving up and down in short vertical motions to mimic the rough texture of bark. Lightly fill in the trunk with the black milk foam. Next, dip a clean etching tool into the pink milk foam and dot some fallen blossom at the base of the tree. Now start building the pink blossom above the trunk by painting in dots, lines and spirals.

For a finishing touch, sprinkle some pretty crushed dried rose petals on top of the blossom.

PENGUIN

Whether you love penguins or are simply seeking a dose of cuteness, this latte art is the perfect choice. Showcasing rosetta pouring skills and a fine etching technique, this charming design is sure to add a touch of whimsy to your morning brew.

1

Prepare two espresso cups of milk foam in black and orange, then set aside. Pour cold fresh milk into a jug and heat to 64–65°C (147–149°F). Pour half the steamed milk into a separate jug and add some navy and black liquid food colouring to create the steel-blue milk. Create the base in a large coffee cup (see page 8).

2

Pour a three-layered tulip (see page 11), starting in the middle of the cup and then pouring to the 6 o'clock position.

Using the blue milk, pour two small rosettas (see page 12) for the wings.

Using an etching tool and the leftover white milk in the jug, outline the penguin's body, dragging from the top to the bottom.

Use a spatula to drop a circle of black milk foam onto the coffee to form the penguin's head.

Dip a fine-tipped tool into the black milk foam and draw the outline of the penguin's pointed beak.

Wipe the etching tool clean and colour in the penguin's neck and beak with the orange milk foam.

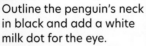

Outline the penguin's neck in black and add a white milk dot for the eye.

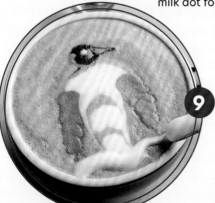

Use a teaspoon handle and white milk left over in the jug to paint the snow that the penguin is standing on.

OCTOPUS

This simple yet colourful design has real impact. It requires just two colours and a small amount of drawing - and takes little more than 3 minutes to achieve. It uses a quenelle of foam to create the 3D shape.

1 Prepare two espresso cups of milk foam in blue and purple, then set aside. To make 'dry foam', steam cold milk to a temperature of 64–65°C (147–149°F), then froth in a jug. Set this to one side for around 30 seconds, allowing the foam to separate above the milk. Create the base in a small coffee cup (see page 8). Then pour the steamed milk slowly and steadily from the main jug into the middle of the cup, to create a circle.

2 To create the octopus's body, place a quenelle of dry foam (see page 8) over the circle, aiming for the middle of the cup.

Using a tablespoon, carefully scoop some dry foam out of the jug and drape it down the sides of the cup to sculpt the octopus's tentacles.

3

4 Use the blue milk foam to colour the spaces between the tentacles and the purple foam to add suction-cup-like details to the tentacles. Be sure to vary the size and spacing of the cups to add realism and depth to the design.

To shape the octopus's head, add a few more quenelles of dry foam on top of the body.

5

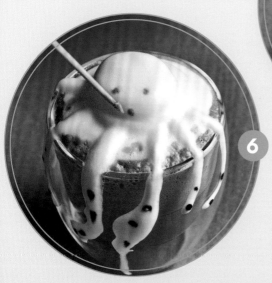

6 Dip a clean fine-tipped etching tool into the corner of the cup, then use the brown crema to paint on the octopus's round eyes and mouth.

WHALE WATCHING

Replicate the wonders of whale watching with this graceful coffee design. Using two short rosettas to create the whale's tail, I would recommend revising the basics on page 12 before giving this design a go.

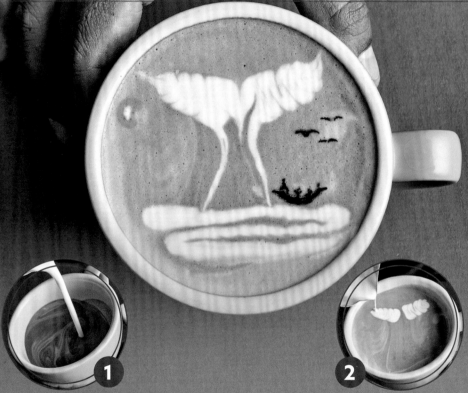

1 Prepare an espresso cup of orange milk foam and another with a small amount of black food colouring. Create the base in a large coffee cup (see page 8), pouring until the cup is two-thirds full.

2 Pour two rosettas diagonally (see page 12), starting in the upper centre of the cup at 12 o'clock and ending near the edge of the cup at 1 o'clock and 11 o'clock.

3

To create the dip in the whale's tail, pour a small heart (see page 10) at the 12 o'clock position, about 2.5cm (1 inch) away from the edge of the cup.

4

Hold the jug over the 8 o'clock position and pour from left to right, then right to left, and back again, moving towards the bottom of the cup. This will create the sea, be it the Arctic, Antarctic or Mediterranean!

5

Use an etching tool to draw two long concave lines to connect the whale's tail with the ocean below. Drag the tips of the whale's tail outwards to add some definition.

6

Use a teaspoon handle to dollop a small circle of orange milk foam in the top-left corner of the cup, to form the sun.

7

Paint the boat and the whale watchers inside with some black food colouring. Then etch some seagulls. As these details are small, a fine etching tool works best.

8

Lastly, add a small white dot within the orange sun, to give it some highlight.

SURFACING
TURTLE

This design is a lovely way to use your tulip and rosetta pouring skills. It can be embellished with as much colour as you wish, although here the colour has been kept to a minimum.

Prepare an espresso cup of blue milk foam and set this to one side. Create the base in a large coffee cup (see page 8), pouring until the cup is one-third full.

2 Start the design as if you're creating a tulip (see page 11) in the centre of the cup, but work to a point for the turtle's body.

Create four small rosettas (see page 12) for the turtle's flippers.

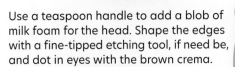

4

Using leftover milk foam and a fine-tipped etching tool, define the edge of the body and connect the flippers.

Use a teaspoon handle to add a blob of milk foam for the head. Shape the edges with a fine-tipped etching tool, if need be, and dot in eyes with the brown crema.

5

6 Use a clean fine-tipped tool and the blue milk foam to etch in waves at the top and bottom of the cup.

PANDA

This bamboo-munching panda uses free pouring for two rosettas and then fine etching to finish. The design features only one panda, but brave baristas might add a second panda to the opposite corner of the cup!

1 Prepare three espresso cups of milk foam in green, brown and black, and set these to one side. Create the base in a large coffee cup (see page 8), pouring until the cup is half-full.

2 With the handle facing away from you, carefully pour two small rosettas (see page 12) to create the panda's paws.

3 Pour a large circle above the paws to create the panda's head.

4 Use a fine-tipped etching tool and black milk foam to outline the head and paws of the panda.

5 Outline the panda's cute little ears in black milk foam, then fill in the paws with black.

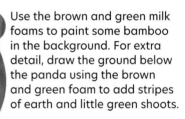

6 Use the brown and green milk foams to paint some bamboo in the background. For extra detail, draw the ground below the panda using the brown and green foam to add stripes of earth and little green shoots.

Outline and fill the eyes with black, then fill the ears and etch the nose and mouth. **7**

8 For a finishing touch, you can draw a piece of bamboo for the panda to chew on. Use a clean etching tool and white milk left over in the jug to add a small white dot to highlight the panda's eyes.

PLANET
EARTH

Using dry foam to build the planet's spherical shape and vibrant food colouring to paint the contrasting continents and oceans, this striking design takes only a few minutes to achieve.

Prepare three espresso cups of milk foam in blue, black and green. Now prepare a jug of dry foam (see page 9) and set this to one side. Next, create the base in a small coffee cup (see page 8). Pour some milk into the centre of the espresso to create a circle, then fill the rest of the cup with milk, leaving a gap of 5mm (¼ inch) at the top.

Using a tablespoon, layer the dry foam over the milk circle to create a 3D dome.

Use an etching tool and the green milk foam to paint over the dry foam and create continents.

Outline the continents and the shape of the Earth with black milk foam. Finally, fill in the sea with blue milk foam. Remember to clean your etching tool whenever you switch colours.

CHAMELEON

As radiant as a sunset, the multi-coloured spines on this sassy chameleon will bring a touch of paradise to any cup.

1 Make sure you have a few different food colourings to hand – shades of green, red, yellow, orange and blue were used for this cup – and set these to one side. Create the base in a large coffee cup (see page 8), filling until the cup is two-thirds full.

2 To create the leaf, pour a slosetta (see page 13) from 9 o'clock to 6 o'clock. When you reach 6 o'clock, lift the jug upwards to create a thin stream, then pour backwards through the slosetta. Continue pouring, beyond the slosetta, until you reach 12 o'clock.

3

To start the chameleon's body, pour a rosetta (see page 12) from 12 o'clock to about 3 o'clock.

4

When you reach 3 o'clock near the handle, keep pouring the milk downwards, then curve left to create the tail.

5

To thicken the body, pour a small, two-layered tulip (see page 11) beneath the rosetta.

6

To create the branch that the chameleon is resting on, pour a horizontal line, starting at 9 o'clock and moving across the cup until you reach the tail.

7

To form the chameleon's head, pour a short vertical line in the top-left corner of the cup, starting at 10 o'clock about 2.5cm (1 inch) away from the edge. Now pour a small spiral to connect this vertical line to the rosetta on the right.

8

To create the front leg, pour downwards diagonally right between the tulip and the chameleon's head, then diagonally left. If you have some leftover milk, you can also add a smaller branch coming off the main branch. Free pour a comma shape, between the first tulip layer and the chameleon's tail to shape the back leg.

9

Use an etching tool and the food colourings to decorate the chameleon's back with lots of vibrant hues. Drag each dot towards the body to blend before going on to the next colour. Clean the etching tool after applying each colour.

SHRIMP

This stunning nautical design uses the tulip in all its glory to create a handsome and amusing artwork.

1 Create the base in a large coffee cup (see page 8), filling until the cup is two-thirds full. For the shrimp's body, pour a four-layered tulip (see page 11), starting in the middle of the cup and ending at 9 o'clock.

2 For the tail, pour a smaller, five-layered tulip under the first, pouring from the 9 o'clock position and diagonally right and downwards.

3

To create the shrimp's head, pour a circle to the right of the first tulip. With a fine-tipped etching tool, manipulate the milk within the head by dragging it outwards. This will form the nose.

4

To shape the tail, turn to the fifth and smallest tulip layer in the lower portion of the shrimp's body. Now, with a clean etching tool, flick the milk within this tulip outwards, creating thin curved lines.

5

Add dots between the two tulips in order to thicken the shrimp's body.

6

Now dip a clean etching tool into the crema and paint on the shrimp's brown eye. Add a white dot of milk inside the eye, to create some highlight. Using leftover white milk from the jug, draw the shrimp's antennae.

7

Outline the shrimp's smile and eyebrow with white milk, then go over the smile with the crema. Use the white milk to draw the shrimp's arms and legs, protruding from the first tulip under the shrimp's head.

8

If the milk has deflated a bit, you can thicken the antennae for a finishing touch.

9

To make the design look more striking, and if you have black food colouring to hand, you might want to outline the whole piece.

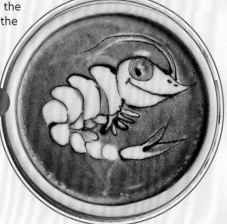

PEACOCK

Combine a tulip with dots of blue and green milk foam to create a majestic peacock flaunting its feathers.

1 Prepare two espresso cups of milk foam in blue and green, and another with a small amount of black food colouring. Create the base in a large coffee cup (see page 8), filling until two-thirds full.

2 To create the body and feathers of the peacock, pour a multi-layered tulip (see pages 16–17), starting from the centre of the cup.

3

To shape the feathers, grip a clean etching tool tightly and use it to drag from the edge of the crema inwards.

4

Use a teaspoon handle to add a circle of blue milk foam to the centre. Move the foam with a fine-tipped etching tool, curving up and slightly round to create the neck.

5

Add a small dollop of blue milk foam at the top of the peacock's neck, to solidify the head.

6

Dot green milk foam around the edges of the feathers to add some bright colour to the tail.

7

Layer blue milk foam on top of the green dots, then add a couple of drops of leftover white milk to the blue dots.

8

With a clean etching tool, drag each dot downwards to create the heart shapes. Drop small blue dots over the tulip, to decorate the feathers.

9

Use a clean fine-tipped etching tool to add the final details. Paint the peacock's beak and eye with the black food colouring. Draw the peacock's crest with more blue milk foam. Pour two vertical lines for legs and use the etching tool to draw the toes.

FOR
ART
LOVERS

WATER LILIES

Imitate the colourful impression of Monet's water-lily series with this enchanting design. Having completed 250 paintings of his water garden, there's no strict layout to this latte art. Be sure to include purples and greens, but feel free to add more colours as you imagine wandering the gardens of Giverny, coffee in hand.

1 Prepare three espresso cups of milk foam in green, orange and purple. Create the base in a single espresso cup (see page 8), pouring until the cup is one-third full.

2 For the background, paint four green dots, positioned as if on an invisible diagonal line from the 9 o'clock to the 12 o'clock position. Draw a line through the dots to join them.

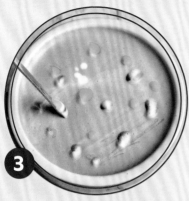

3

Use a teaspoon handle to splatter dots of green milk foam across the surface of the coffee, to form the lily pads. Stripe the purple milk foam with a dollop of white milk foam, then use this new colour combination to blob on some more dots.

4

Use a clean etching tool to drag across all the dots in a zigzag motion to complete the background for the water lilies.

5

Using a teaspoon, dollop small blobs of white milk foam at the 5 o'clock, 8 o'clock, 11 o'clock and 3 o'clock positions, to form the lily pads. Add two smaller circles near the centre of the coffee, to start the water lily flowers.

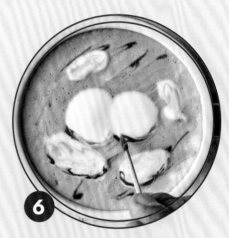

6

Using a fine-tipped etching tool, colour the lily pads in green. Outline the bottom of the water lily flowers and the lower lily pads in purple.

7

To create the petals for the water lily flowers, manipulate the milk by dragging from the centre of each flower outwards. This will spike the previously smooth, circular outline.

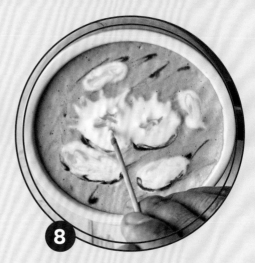

8

With the orange milk foam, draw the stamen in the middle of each flower.

9

If the lily pads have lost some colour, use a clean tool to top them up with green milk foam to make them appear more vibrant.

10

Go over the outline of the lily pads in places to finish this art-inspired design.

THE STARRY NIGHT

Painted in 1889, Vincent Van Gogh's *The Starry Night* is one of the most famous paintings in the world. Now, with the judicious use of milk foam in three colours, you can recreate it on the surface of your favourite hot drink.

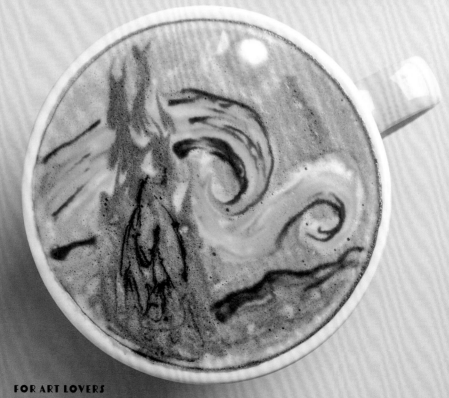

Prepare three espresso cups of milk foam in blue, black and orange. Pour fresh cold milk into a jug and heat it to 64–65°C (147-149°F). Use a spoon or spatula to stripe this milk with some blue food colouring. Create the base in a large coffee cup (see page 8), pouring until the cup is two-thirds full.

Starting at the 9 o'clock position, draw a spiral with the blue milk in the jug by moving your wrist in a circular motion. Draw a second spiral from inside the first outwards to the right.

Outline the spirals with the blue milk foam, using an etching tool.

Wipe the tool and use the black milk foam to paint the cypress trees in the foreground. Draw more spirals with the blue milk foam between the trees and the sky.

Use a teaspoon handle to paint the moon with the orange milk foam.

Use white milk foam to add a highlight to the moon, then use a fine-tipped etching tool to add small orange circles around the edge of the cup. These are the stars.

THE PERSISTENCE OF MEMORY

Plunge into the mind-bending realm of Salvador Dalí's *The Persistence of Memory* with this design, featuring surreal soft clocks and watches that melt from your own cup.

1 Make three espresso cups of milk foam in blue, green and black. Create the base in a big coffee cup (see page 8) until two-thirds full.

2 For the first clock, pour a heart (see page 10) above the 7 o'clock point, about 2.5cm (1 inch) away from the edge of the cup. Next, pour a line of white milk from around 10 o'clock to 1 o'clock. This is the sky.

3

Etch the watch and sky with blue milk foam and add green milk foam to the sky.

4

Outline the watch with the black milk foam. Then draw a tree trunk to the left of the watch.

5

To create the second melting watch, dollop a circle of white milk just above the centre of the cup. Then colour the second watch with the blue milk foam.

6

Use the black milk foam to paint a clock face onto both watches. As these are small details, a clean fine-tipped etching tool would work best.

7

Go over the outline of the large melting watch with the black milk foam.

8

Use a soup spoon to scoop up the large watch and drop it gently over the side of the cup to create the melting effect.

THE
SCREAM

The painting of a tortured face by Edvard Munch is one of the most iconic images in art and a fun one to reproduce. Here only one colour has been used, so you can concentrate on getting the figure right and keep the background plain. You can use blues, yellows and oranges to paint the background if you wish, but don't let your coffee get cold!

1 Prepare an espresso cup of black milk foam. Create the base in a large coffee cup (see page 8), pouring until the cup is half-full.

2 Pour fresh cold milk into a jug and heat to 64–65°C (147–149°F). Froth the milk to create a dry foam (see page 9). Pour a milk circle for the head, then drag the milk left to right in a crescent for the body and arms.

3 Using a spatula, layer the dry foam onto the circle and add a little to the body and arms. Tidy up the outlines with an etching tool.

Using the spatula, drag upwards from the body on either side of the head to create the rest of the man's arms and the hands.

4

5

Use the black milk foam to draw the shirt and fill it in.

6

Draw the eyes, mouth and nostrils with the black milk foam. Add some texture in the background using a fine-tipped tool.

MONA LISA

If you're going to have artworks on your coffee, then go for the most famous of all - Leonardo da Vinci's *La Giaconda*! To etch on the Mona Lisa would take some time (Leonardo's coffee would have gone cold if he did it this way), so we've provided you with a stencil for the key elements.

1 Prepare two espresso cups of milk foam in blue and green, and another with a small amount of black food colouring. Create the base in a large coffee cup (see page 8), filling the cup until you are 3mm (⅛ inch) from the top.

Place the *Mona Lisa* stencil (see page 124) on top of the cup, ensuring it doesn't touch the coffee. If need be, bend the stencil slightly, so it curves away from the surface. Ideally, each part should be an even distance away. Support the finer parts with cocktail sticks. 2

3 Gently dust chocolate powder all over the stencil to create the outline of the hair and clothes.

4 Paint in the face with black food colouring, paying particular attention to that enigmatic smile! You can add the detail of the hands if you like, but I don't think you need to and the chocolate will deteriorate and 'bubble' the longer you leave it.

5 Use the blue and green milk foams to add some colour to the sides of the cup and give an impression of the rest of the painting.

THE BIRTH OF VENUS

This simple, yet effective design is based on Botticelli's famous painting. It is little more than four easy steps and can be as detailed as you wish. Feel free to experiment with different coloured chocolate powder.

1 Prepare an espresso cup of orange milk foam and set this aside. Create the base in a large coffee cup (see page 8), pouring until the cup is two-thirds full.

2 Pour a tulip (see page 11) along the bottom of the cup, pouring to one side. Fill the cup, but leave a 3mm (⅛ inch) space at the top, so the stencil won't touch the coffee.

3 Place the *Birth of Venus* stencil (see page 124) on top of the cup, ensuring it doesn't touch the surface of the coffee. If need be, bend the stencil slightly, so it curves away from the surface. Dust the stencil generously with chocolate powder.

4 Use an etching tool and the orange milk foam to draw on Venus's flowing hair.

THE SON OF MAN

You may be familiar with *The Son of Man*, a surrealist painting by René Magritte, but have you seen it on coffee? Amuse art enthusiasts with this remarkable design, combining the free pouring of double hearts with etching.

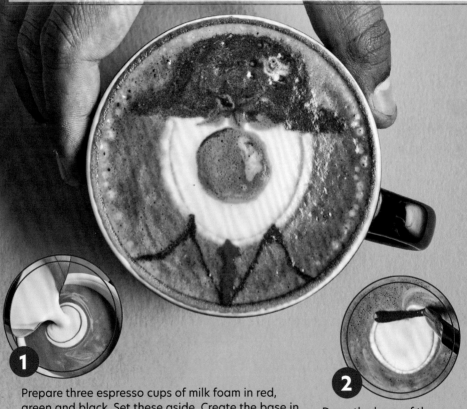

1 Prepare three espresso cups of milk foam in red, green and black. Set these aside. Create the base in a small coffee cup (see page 8), filling the cup until two-thirds full. Pour a double heart (see page 14) in the centre of the cup, but instead of dragging a thin stream of milk all the way down at the end, only drag downwards slightly, to leave a circular shape.

2 Draw the base of the hat with the black milk foam. The handle of a tablespoon or a small spatula will work best.

3

Outline the rest of the hat in black and fill it in.

4 Dollop a circle of green milk foam in the middle of the double heart to create the apple. Use an etching tool to smooth the outline of the apple, if necessary.

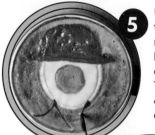

5 Use a fine-tipped etching tool and black milk foam to etch the shirt underneath the double heart. You need to draw a central V-shape first, then a diagonal line from the top of the 'V' on both sides, moving downwards left and right, to shape the shoulders. To guide you, the bottom of the 'V' should sit at the 6 o'clock position and the top of the 'V' should rest against the double heart.

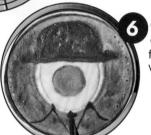

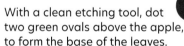

6 Clean the etching tool, then outline a tie with the red milk foam in the middle of the central V-shape and colour it in.

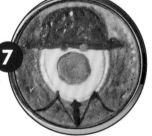

With a clean etching tool, dot two green ovals above the apple, to form the base of the leaves.

7

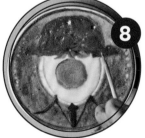

8 Drag the middle of each green oval, pulling the milk outwards to create a leaf shape. Add a couple more green leaves, if you wish.

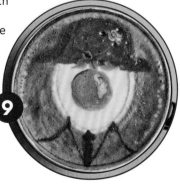

9

For a finishing touch, use leftover white milk to highlight the apple and hat.

MONUMENTS

TAJ MAHAL

Mesmerize family and friends as India's most famous landmark materializes on the surface of their morning coffee. This is an advanced design that uses rosettas, a slosetta and heart to complete.

1

Prepare two espresso cups of milk foam in blue and green, and set aside. Create the base in a large coffee cup (see page 8), filling the cup two-thirds full. Pour a slosetta (see page 13) from the centre of the cup to the 6 o'clock position. This is the water in front of the Taj Mahal.

2

To create the minarets, pour two rosettas (see page 12) from the centre of the cup to the 11 o'clock and 1 o'clock positions. Make these thinner than the slosetta and begin pouring level with the start of the slosetta.

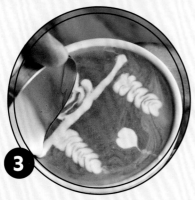

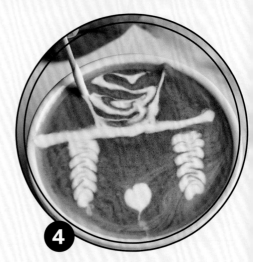

3

To form the main dome, pour a small heart (see page 10) 2.5cm (1 inch) away from the edge of the cup, at 12 o'clock. Pour a horizontal line beneath the two rosettas, across the width of the cup.

4

Dip an etching tool into the white milk left over in the jug and draw two diagonal lines on either side of the slosetta to outline the water.

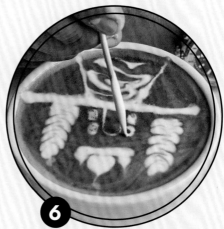

5

Add two dots either on side of the dome with a tablespoon handle. Next, manipulate the milk by flicking each dot upwards with a fine-tipped etching tool. This will help shape the domed kiosks. Draw a white line under the dome and the two kiosks.

6

Outline the main arch above the slosetta. Now etch two windows either side of the arch with leftover white milk. As these are fine details, a skewer or cocktail stick would work best.

7

Draw a vertical line either side of the four windows as walls, meeting the short horizonal line beneath the heart and forming the outline of the building.

8

Draw a second short horizontal line beneath the first, under the domed kiosks. Use the tablespoon handle and white milk from the jug to thicken the building's walls.

9

Add some detail to the top of both minarets by dragging milk from each rosetta upwards to create a point. Now dip a clean etching tool into the crema and sharpen the lines of each rosetta.

10

Swirl blue and green milk foam with a clean etching tool in the water. Paint little trees either side of the water and rosettas, using green milk foam for the leaves and leftover white milk for the trunks. Add two smaller kiosks in white milk next to the first two.

EIFFEL TOWER

The perfect way to impress all the Francophiles in your life, with just one sip this coffee art will whisk you to the magic and romance of Paris.

1 Prepare two espresso cups of milk foam in yellow and orange, then set aside. Create the base in a large coffee cup (see page 8).

2 To form the supports, pour two diagonal rosettas (see page 12), starting in the centre of the cup and moving outwards to the 5 o'clock and 7 o'clock positions.

3

Pour a third vertical rosetta, starting where the first two rosettas meet. Then raise the jug to create a thin stream of milk, pouring until you reach the 12 o'clock position and dragging down slightly at the end.

4

Use a teaspoon handle or etching tool and leftover white milk from the jug to sharpen the edges of the rosetta and tidy up the outline.

5

Using a teaspoon handle as a paintbrush, draw the first platform of the Eiffel Tower.

6

Use an etching tool to add a blob of white milk to create the top platform. Tidy up this outline, if needed, with a clean etching tool.

7

Draw a white, curved line just below the first platform to improve the shape at the bottom.

8

Using a clean etching tool, decorate the design with yellow milk foam, however you choose. Here, I coloured in the top platform and added dots throughout.

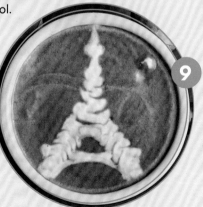

9

Add a moon in the top-right corner of the cup, dolloping on a circle of orange milk foam and then adding white milk over the top to highlight.

LIBERTY'S TORCH

Dazzle your friends with this caffeine-powered tribute to Lady Liberty. Showcasing rosettas and a fine etching technique, this design will infuse your coffee with grandeur and a touch of American pride.

1 Prepare an espresso cup of orange milk foam and set this to one side. Add turquoise food colouring to some milk, then steam and froth this. Use this turquoise colour for the base (see page 8), filling the cup until two-thirds full.

2 Pour the first rosetta (see page 12), starting in the centre of the cup and finishing at the 6 o'clock position. This will be the handle of the torch.

3

To create Lady Liberty's arm, pour a second rosetta, this time starting in the centre and moving diagonally to end at the 7 o'clock position.

4

Pour a third rosetta horizontally just above the torch's handle. This should be much shorter than the first two.

5

Using leftover turquoise milk from the jug, use an etching tool to carefully draw two concave lines, connecting the third rosetta to the first two. Then draw a shallow curved line above the third rosetta to add detail to the torch.

6

Use the handle end of a tablespoon to dollop a small circle of turquoise milk above the second rosetta, to shape Lady Liberty's hand.

7

Clean the spoon, then dollop a circle of orange milk foam above the torch to add fire.

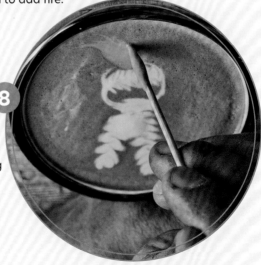

8

Sharpen the petals of the third rosetta with a clean fine-tipped etching tool. This should create the appearance of a string of squashed arrow shapes, pointing towards 9 o'clock. Now use a clean etching tool to manipulate the milk within the fire, dragging the orange circle outwards to create curved, elongated flames.

TOWER BRIDGE

In contrast to London's original Tower Bridge, which took 8 years to build, you'll be able to enjoy this slosetta-structured replica in just a few minutes.

1 Prepare an espresso cup of blue milk foam and set this to one side. Create the base in a large coffee cup (see page 8), filling the cup two-thirds full.

2 Pour two straight slosettas (see page 13) from the lower centre of the cup, between 8 o'clock and 11 o'clock, and then 4 o'clock and 1 o'clock.

3

Pour a horizontal line beneath the slosettas to create the base of the bridge.

4

Use an etching tool to outline the slosettas with leftover white milk and add V-shaped turrets. Draw the footway and suspenders.

5

Paint the drawbridge with white milk by adding two short diagonal lines between the slosettas above the base.

6

Dip an etching tool into the white milk, then move it back and forth to create a shallow zigzag underneath the bridge. This will be the river.

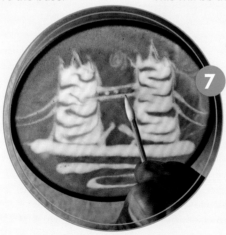

7

Decorate the bridge with blue and white milk foam, however you choose. Here, I coloured in the tops of the towers and added dots along the upper footway. I also added vertical cables beneath the suspenders.

FOR OCCASIONS

SNOWMAN

Turn an ordinary cup of coffee into a winter wonderland with this whimsical snowman design. I've added a touch of orange for the moon and the carrot nose, but why stop there? Let your creativity shine by colouring in the trees or dressing the snowman in some stylish winter attire.

1 Prepare an espresso cup of orange milk foam and another with a small amount of black food colouring, then set aside. Create the base in a large coffee cup (see page 8), pouring to two-thirds full.

2 Pour a straight rosetta (see page 12), starting at the 8 o'clock position and finishing at 10 o'clock.

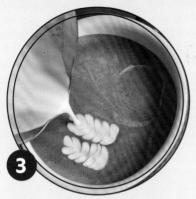

3

Pour a second rosetta to the right of the first, to create the trees in the landscape.

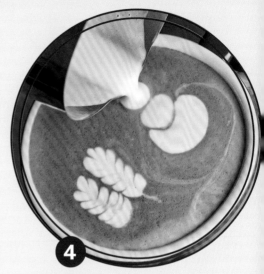

4

For the snowman, pour a three-layered tulip (see page 11), starting near the handle and ending at 1 o'clock. Omit the last step to keep the tulip layers more rounded.

5

Use a teaspoon handle to etch the ground beneath the rosetta trees and tulip snowman with leftover white milk from the jug, moving from left to right across the cup.

6

Use more leftover white milk from the jug to paint on the tree trunks.

7

Dip an etching tool into the white milk and paint on a clump of grass, dragging upwards from the ground in short vertical strokes. A fine-tipped tool etching works best, as the grass is quite small.

8

Clean the etching tool and dip it into the brown crema to draw on the snowman's face and buttons.

9

Use the orange milk foam to draw the snowman's carrot nose. Now use a clean fine-tipped tool to manipulate the milk to form arms, pulling from the second tulip layer outwards. Dot on the hands with white milk.

10

Use the orange milk foam to dot the moon in the top-left corner of the cup. Lastly, use the white milk to add some flakes of falling snow to the scene.

VALENTINE'S BEAR

It's not just about making your loved one a morning coffee on Valentine's Day; it's about adding an adorable design to the crema! How about this cuddly teddy bear, holding a romantic red heart? For a personal touch, feel free to etch in your loved one's initials in milk foam on the heart.

1 Prepare an espresso cup of red milk foam and a second with a small amount of black food colouring. Create the base in a small coffee cup (see page 8), filling until two-thirds full.

2 Carefully pour a double heart (see page 14) in the lower centre of the cup near the 6 o'clock position.

3

Pour a circle just above the heart, to form the bear's head.

4

Pour two little paws on either side of the double heart, at the 9 o'clock and 3 o'clock positions.

5

Use a teaspoon handle to dollop on two white circles above the head to shape the ears.

6

Dip an etching tool into the crema, then use this to outline the double heart and paint the bear's snout.

7

With the brown crema, dot on the eyes and draw the nose and mouth.

8

Add a dot of crema to each ear and add small stripes to the paws to etch the bear's claws.

9

Colour the inner heart with the red milk foam, using a clean teaspoon handle. Lastly, tidy any outlines with a clean etching tool, if necessary.

EASTER CHICK

Hop into the spirit of Easter with this delightful design. Featuring a vibrant yellow hue to brighten even the dreariest of mornings, this cheerful chick is bound to put a smile on your face.

1. Prepare two espresso cups of milk foam in yellow and orange, and a third cup with a small amount of black food colouring. Set these to one side. Create the base in a large coffee cup (see page 8), filling the cup until it is two-thirds full.

2 Pour three short rosettas (see page 12) to form a loose triangle shape in the lower central portion of the cup. Make sure that the ends of each rosetta don't touch. Now pour a circle above the rosettas to form the chick's head.

3 Dollop some extra milk with a tablespoon on top of the circle to connect the head with the rosettas. Next, dip a fine-tipped etching tool into the white milk foam left over in the jug and outline the chick's shell.

4 With a clean etching tool, outline the whole design with the black food colouring, adding extra details to the chick's shell if you wish.

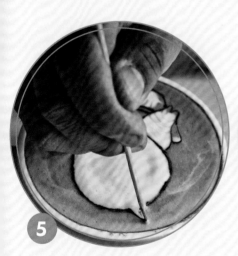

5 Carefully colour in the chick's head with the yellow milk foam and create some fluff on the top. Do this by dragging the yellow milk foam outwards. Then outline the cute fluff with some black food colouring.

6 Dot on the beak with orange milk foam, then shape and outline the edges with black. Add the black eyes and eyebrows. Paint stripes on the wings with yellow milk foam and add white dots between the wings. Always clean the tool when you change colours.

SHAMROCK

You've probably seen the iconic symbol of Ireland poured onto the head of a Guinness, but have you ever imagined it gracing the surface of your coffee? It's time to bring the luck of the Irish to your morning brew with this simple St Patrick's Day design.

Prepare an espresso cup of green milk foam and set this to one side. Make a jug of dry foam (see page 9). To mimic the colour of Guinness beer, prepare an Americano in a small coffee cup.

2

Pour the dry foam to create the Guinness froth, starting from the centre and spiralling outwards to form a circle. Use a clean etching tool to tidy the outline of the circle, if necessary.

3

Use a teaspoon to dollop on three circles of the green milk foam to create the leaves in the centre of the cup.

4

Using a fine etching tool, drag from the edge of each leaf towards the middle of the clover. This will add definition to the shamrock design.

5

Lastly, draw the stem of the clover underneath the leaves using the green milk foam.

RAINBOW FOR
PRIDE

Celebrate Pride in style with this delightful coffee art. A heart and some bright food colouring can result in an impressive, but simple, design.

1

Add blue food colouring to milk, then steam and froth before setting to one side in an espresso cup. Repeat for the red, yellow and green colours. Create the base in a small coffee cup (see page 8), filling nearly to the brim.

2

Use a teaspoon to dollop a circle of red milk in the centre of the cup.

3

Clean the teaspoon, then dollop a circle of yellow milk on top of the red.

4

Next, add a circle of green to the yellow.

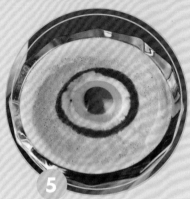

5

Dollop a circle of blue on top of the green.

6

With a clean etching tool, draw a line through the centre of the circle to create a heart shape.

7

For an optional extra flourish, add small stripes around the heart with the different colours, spinning the cup around carefully to blend them a little.

HANUKKAH

Let this captivating menorah design become a part of your Hanukkah traditions, bringing a touch of joy, light and beauty to the festivities.

1 Make two espresso cups of milk foam in yellow and red, then set aside. Create the base in a large coffee cup (see page 8).

2 Pour a multi-layered tulip (see pages 16-17) with five layers in the centre of the cup. Before you finish pouring, drag the jug from right to left to create a straight line to cut off the tulip and form an arch.

Blob a small circle of milk above the middle of the tulip. This will form the base for the central candle. Dip a clean etching tool into the crema, then outline the central support of the menorah by dragging down over the tulip.

Using a teaspoon handle, paint the menorah stand in a triangular shape and fill this in with leftover white milk.

Use an etching tool to add eight small circles along the top of the tulip. These will be the lamps. You can add dots along the central support for added detail.

With a fine-tipped etching tool, paint the row of candlesticks as short vertical lines in red milk foam above each lamp.

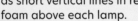

Use a clean etching tool to add dots of yellow milk foam to the end of each candlestick. Drag upwards from the centre of these dots to create the effect of flames.

Use the rest of the yellow milk foam to add highlights to the central support of the menorah, the eight branches and also the stand.

HOLI

Celebrate the Hindu festival of colours, love and spring with this vibrant and exhilarating design! Brighten up your cup with bursts of red, blue, green and yellow, and even layer powdered food colouring on top.

1 Prepare four espresso cups of milk foam in blue, yellow, green and red, then set aside. Fill another cup with a small amount of black food colouring. Create the base in a large coffee cup (see page 8), filling until the cup is two-thirds full.

2 Pour a rosetta (see page 12), starting above the 7 o'clock position and pouring downwards until you reach the cup edge.

3 Pour three more rosettas to the right of the first. Dollop a small circle of milk above each rosetta, then shape to create the outstretched hands.

4 Use a fine-tipped etching tool to paint the fingers and thumbs, changing the colours for some hands.

5 Add some green dots, using a teaspoon handle for precision.

6 Add red dots, blue dots, and yellow dots too.

7 Use a clean etching tool to drag through the dots, moving in diagonal lines to blur them. This will mimic the colourful chaos of paint thrown into the air.

8 To finish, use a large spoon to sprinkle powdered food colourings over the design. Use a clean etching tool to outline the raised arms with the black food colouring.

SUPERNATURAL

ZOMBIE

With green slime, bulging eyes and a missing nose, this creation is the ghastliest yet! Although the design requires little pouring, you will need precise etching skills to bring this zombie to life. Make sure you have a fine-tipped etching tool to master the trickiest details.

1 Prepare an espresso cup of green milk foam and one with a small amount of black food colouring. Create the base in a large coffee cup (see page 8).

2 To start the head, pour an oval in the centre of the cup. Use a teaspoon to layer milk on top of the oval to create the skull shape.

3

Use a fine-tipped etching tool to outline the skull neatly with the green milk foam.

4

Colour the skull in green, moving the tool in spiralling motions to add texture as you do so. Clean the etching tool and outline the nose with white milk.

5

With a fine-tipped tool, draw on the lips of the zombie with the white milk leftover in the pitcher. Use a teaspoon handle to dot on the zombie's eyes.

6

To create the melting effect, manipulate the white milk of each eye. Do this by dragging a clean etching tool upwards through the eyes and spiking the circle shape. Here I dragged through each eye three times, forming a sideways E-shape.

7 Add some white dots inside the mouth to create the zombie's teeth. Then use a clean fine-tipped etching tool to fill the inside of the mouth with some black food colouring.

8 Dip the tool into the black food colouring and outline the eyes, nose and mouth.

9 Colour the nose in black – this will make it look hollowed out. Next, paint slime over the skull by dotting around the face with green milk foam. Now drag each dot downwards to give the appearance of dripping slime.

10 Add bags underneath the zombie's eyes with black food colouring and also outline the drops of slime to finish the design.

WIZARD

Whether you're a fan of Dumbledore's wise counsel or Gandalf's epic adventures, this coffee art creation will add a touch of magic to your morning. Using three rosettas to form the hat and beard, this mysterious wizard is the perfect design for the fantasy-readers in your life.

1
Add purple food colouring to an espresso cup. Create the base in a small coffee cup (see page 8).

2
Begin shaping the wizard's pointy hat by pouring a rosetta (see page 12). Start in the centre of the cup and move upwards to finish at the 12 o'clock position.

3

To create the wizard's beard, pour a second rosetta, starting centre left and curving downwards to around 6 o'clock. Pour a third rosetta, starting centre right and curving downwards to meet the previous rosetta.

To form the base of the wizard's hat, pour a horizontal line from left to right beneath the first rosetta.

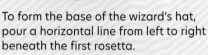

4

5

Dip a fine-tipped etching tool in the white milk and thicken the base of the hat. Outline the rosetta, adding a curved point to the top of the hat.

Use an etching tool to flick the milk in each rosetta outwards slightly and drag to the side or down. This will give the beard and hat some textured detail.

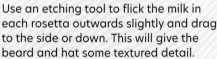

6

7

Use white milk to add the wizard's nose, moustache and mouth inside the beard. Add one eye to suggest that the wizard is winking.

8

For a finishing touch, use the purple colouring to add a ribbon to the hat.

DRAGON

By skillfully combining three rosettas with a touch of expert etching, a magnificent fire-breather will emerge on the surface of your cup. For those looking for a little more vibrancy, add some colour to the milk before steaming, to create a dragon in whatever hue you choose.

1 Prepare three espresso cups of milk foam in orange, red and yellow. Create the base in a large coffee cup (see page 8), filling until two-thirds full. Pour a rosetta (see page 12) to create the neck, starting in the centre of the cup and finishing at 3 o'clock.

2 For the jaw, add two smaller rosettas, pouring from the centre upwards and then downwards.

3 Use an etching tool to carefully outline the bottom of the dragon's jaw and neck with the orange milk foam.

4 Use the red milk foam to draw spirals for the dragon's whiskers.

5 Wipe the etching tool clean and blob on a small circle of yellow milk foam to form the dragon's eye. Use the milk left over in the jug to add a small white blob inside the yellow circle. This will highlight the eye.

Using clean white milk, drag the etching tool inside the dragon's jaw to create the teeth.

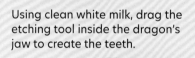

6

7 Use a clean etching tool and the red milk foam to draw spirals to look like fire coming out of the dragon's mouth.

GHOST

Add a touch of spookiness to your morning brew at Hallowe'en with this supernatural creation. For beginners who have not yet mastered the rosetta, leave out steps 2 and 3 and create a ghost without a background.

1 Fill an espresso cup with a small amount of black food colouring. Create the base in a large coffee cup (see page 8), pouring until it is two-thirds full.

2 Pour a rosetta (see page 12), starting roughly at the 4 o'clock position and finishing at 7 o'clock.

3 Now pour a second rosetta so that it is sitting directly above the first one.

4 To shape the ghost's head, pour a circle of white milk 2.5cm (1 inch) away from the edge of the cup, at around 10 o'clock.

5 Use a tablespoon to dollop a curved line of milk to connect the ghost's head with the rosettas.

6 Add a second curved line next to the first, to create the ghost's tail.

7 Add two more lines to fill out the tail, then use the back of a tablespoon to shape and smudge the tail to create a floating effect.

8 Use a clean fine-tipped etching tool to draw on the ghost's face with the black food colouring.

UNICORN

Master the art of free pouring with this enchanting silhouette. Bringing delight to both the young and young-at-heart, I would recommend using a hot chocolate base (see page 123) when serving this design to children.

1 Create the base in a large cup (see page 8), filling until it is two-thirds full. Pour a rosetta (see page 12) from the centre of the cup to the 1 o'clock position. This will be the wings.

2 For the neck, pour a second rosetta to the left of the first, starting in the centre of the cup and ending at 12 o'clock. Before finishing this rosetta, drag the milk slightly to the left to shape the head.

To create the unicorn's body, pour a third rosetta. For this one, you will need to turn your cup so the rosetta is perpendicular to the first two. Starting beneath the second rosetta, pour to the right until you are beneath the first. Continue pouring up the side of the first rosetta and down again, but raise the jug to create a thin stream. This will be the tail.

Pour downwards to create the back legs, from the third rosetta on the right side of the cup.

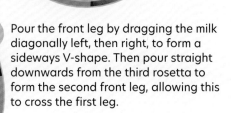

Pour the front leg by dragging the milk diagonally left, then right, to form a sideways V-shape. Then pour straight downwards from the third rosetta to form the second front leg, allowing this to cross the first leg.

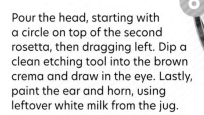

Pour the head, starting with a circle on top of the second rosetta, then dragging left. Dip a clean etching tool into the brown crema and draw in the eye. Lastly, paint the ear and horn, using leftover white milk from the jug.

MERMAID

Showcasing an advanced tulip pouring technique, this design is sure to bring a touch of underwater magic to your morning coffee.

1

Create the base in a large coffee cup (see page 8), filling the cup until it is one-third full.

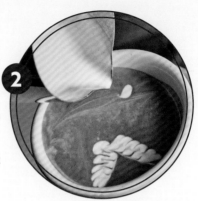

2

Starting 2.5cm (1 inch) away from the edge of the cup at 3 o'clock, pour a rosetta (see page 12) diagonally upwards and right, ending at around 2 o'clock. Pour a second rosetta upwards at a steeper angle, starting just left of the first rosetta and ending at around 1 o'clock. This will be the mermaid's tail.

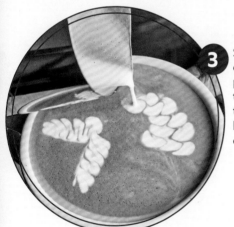

3

Starting 2.5cm (1 inch) from the cup at the 9 o'clock position, pour tulips (see page 11) round the cup until they connect with tail. Repeatedly twist the jug left, then right, when pouring and ensure the tulips narrow.

4

Pour a circle to create the mermaid's head. Using an etching tool, paint on the mermaid's hair with leftover white milk from the jug. Lastly, outline the mermaid's tail to add some definition.

MODERN LEISURE AND LIVING

GLAMOROUS EYE

Perfect your etching skills with this glamorous eye design. Here I've used blue food colouring for the makeup, but feel free to combine whatever colours you choose.

1 Prepare an espresso cup of blue milk foam and two others with a small amount of black and red food colouring. Create the base in a large coffee cup (see page 8), filling until two-thirds full.

2 Use a teaspoon handle to add a short horizontal line, positioned in the lower central part of the cup.

3 To start the eye, manipulate the milk within this line, to create an almond shape. Now extend the corners by dragging slightly outwards.

Use a fine-tipped etching tool to outline the eyelid and eyebrow with white milk. Go over the eyelid lines with blue milk foam, then fill in the eyeshadow in blue.

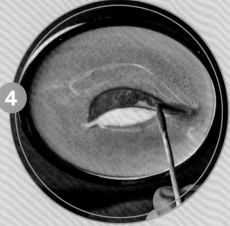

4

5 Next, add a line of blue eyeshadow to the lower lid.

Outline the eyebrow with the blue milk foam and then fill it in.

6

7 Line the eye with the black food colouring, paint on some black eyelashes and add the pupil.

Colour in the iris with the blue milk foam. **8**

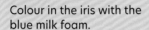

9 Add red food colouring to the corners of the eye and eyebrow. Use a clean fine-tipped etching tool and black food colouring to add hair strands to the eyebrow, smudging a bit to smooth.

To finish the design, dot white gems on the eyeshadow with leftover milk from the jug. **10**

FOOTBALL

Here is a 'striking' design for the sports fan in your life that uses a simple stencil on top of a clever background.

1 Create the base in a large coffee cup (see page 8), pouring until the cup is two-thirds full.

2 Pour six to ten tulips (see page 11) from the side of the cup, rotating the cup as you go.

Pour the milk into the centre so it draws the tulips together to form a wheel. Leave a space of at least 3mm (⅛ inch) at the top to allow a large enough gap for the stencil to sit on top.

3

4 Spin the cup on the work surface to create a whirl around the edge of the wheel.

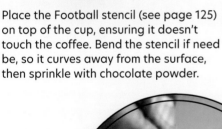

Place the Football stencil (see page 125) on top of the cup, ensuring it doesn't touch the coffee. Bend the stencil if need be, so it curves away from the surface, then sprinkle with chocolate powder.

5

6 Use a teaspoon to add a big blob of milk foam at the end of the player's foot to create the football, sketching in details of the ball with some crema, if you wish.

RACEHORSE

Whether you're an equestrian enthusiast or simply appreciate the artistry involved, this impressive design uses rosettas and bent limbs to bring the thrill of the racetrack to the surface of your cup.

1 Add a small amount of black food colouring to an espresso cup, then set this to one side. Create the base in a large coffee cup (see page 8), pouring until the cup is two-thirds full.

2 Pour two rosettas (see page 12), one along the bottom of the cup to form the ground and the other slightly smaller, about two-thirds of the way up the cup for the horse's body.

Pour a small, tapering rosetta at one end of the body rosetta to begin the head.

Pour the legs, one at the back of the body and two at the front.

Pour the rest of the head, moving from the top down towards the nose and back around the jaw line, leaving a circle of brown crema showing for the eye.

Use a teaspoon handle to add milk foam left over from the jug for the tail.

Add the edge of the other back leg using a fine-tipped etching tool.

Use the handle end of the teaspoon again to add milk foam to form the rider.

Add the helmet with the black food colouring using a clean fine-tipped tool. You can add reins and boots, but I think the design is effective without.

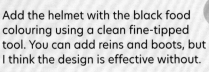

AMERICAN FOOTBALL
HELMET

Here's a fun one for game day: why not create you favourite team's helmet for a good-luck morning latte? You can choose the colours of your team, but be warned...if you do this and they win, then you'll have to do it every time they play!

Prepare espresso cups of coloured milk foam to match your team's logo. Create the base in a large coffee cup (see page 8), pouring until the cup is two-thirds full.

If you like, pour two rosettas (see page 12) at the bottom of the cup, one from the 5 o'clock position to 3 o'clock and the other from 7 o'clock to 9 o'clock. This adds a little background to the helmet.

Place the Helmet stencil (see page 125) on top of the cup, ensuring it doesn't touch the surface of the coffee. Bend the stencil if need be, so it curves away from the surface. You may need to support the 'logo circle' with a cocktail stick. Dust generously with chocolate powder.

Lift the stencil off and add a big red blob (or whatever colour represents your team) of milk foam to the side of the helmet as the logo.

Use a fine-tipped etching tool to outline the logo in white, adding team details, if you wish.

Outline the grid of the helmet guard in white foam and add a blob of foam for the ear hole.

YOGA POSE

Why not present the yoga fan in your life with some yogic coffee art? I've added some background detail, but you could simply use the stencil provided to make a quick impression.

1 Create the base in a large coffee cup (see page 8), pouring until it is two-thirds full. Pour the first layer of a multi-layered tulip (see pages 16–17) in the top-left corner of the cup.

As you pour, make sure that the petals are thicker and closer together than usual. Finish pouring the rest of the tulip. This represents the sun.

2

3 Pour two rosettas (see page 12), one from the 5 o'clock position to 2 o'clock and the other from 7 o'clock to 10 o'clock, to create two trees either side of the person. Add a line between the two to represent the floor.

4 Place the Yoga stencil (see page 126) on top of the cup with the silhouette's feet on the 'floor'. Ensure the stencil doesn't touch the surface of the coffee. Bend the stencil if need be, so it curves away from the surface. Dust with lots of chocolate powder.

5 Lift off the stencil to reveal the 'yogicized' coffee!

DIVER

Make a splash with your coffee design by adding this simple stencil diver.

1

Create the base in a large coffee cup (see page 8), pouring until the cup is two-thirds full.

To create the splash, slow pour a rosetta (see page 12), pouring the milk back and forth from about halfway up the cup towards the 6 o'clock position.

2

3

Use a fine-tipped etching tool to take some milk foam and flick it towards the centre of the rosetta in order to create splashes.

4

5

Lift off the stencil to reveal your diver.

Place the Diver stencil (see page 126) on top of the cup, ensuring it doesn't touch the coffee. Bend the stencil if need be, so it curves away from the surface. Dust generously with chocolate powder.

SAXOPHONE

Jazz up your morning routine with this sleek musical design. Feel free to use yellow milk, for a realistic look, or add different colours to the keys for a more playful touch.

1 Prepare two espresso cups of milk foam in blue and orange, then set these to one side. Create the base in a large coffee cup (see page 8), pouring until the cup is two-thirds full.

2 Pour a rosetta (see page 12), starting from the 9 o'clock position, about 2.5cm (1 inch) away from the edge of the cup, and finishing at 7 o'clock to create the bell of the saxophone.

To create the saxophone body, pour a second rosetta, this time starting at 7 o'clock and ending at 1 o'clock. Drag the milk to the right when pouring the last part of this rosetta to form the mouthpiece. **3**

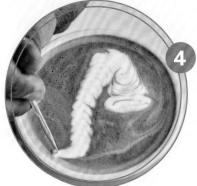

4 Draw a large ellipse at the end of the bell and a smaller one on the mouthpiece, using leftover milk from the jug.

Use the blue milk foam to draw on the musical notes. **5**

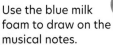

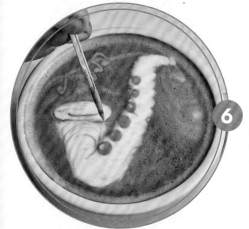

6 Finally, use the orange milk foam to dot on the keys and highlight the opening of the bell.

MUSICAL
STAVE

Hot chocolate powder can be used to create coffee art effectively.
This is a quick way to impress any music lover on a cold evening.

Mix enough hot chocolate powder with steamed milk to give a thick chocolate cream. Pour this into a squeezy bottle and set aside. Prepare a double espresso and pour this into a shot glass. Pour fresh cold milk into a jug and heat it to 64–65°C (147-149°F), then pour into a coffee cup, filling two-thirds full.

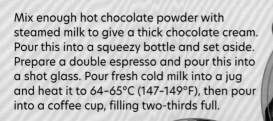

1

2

Pour some espresso foam over the coffee, dragging from 9 o'clock to 3 o'clock across the cup to create a crema on top.

3

Using the hot chocolate in the squeezy bottle, draw on the stave.

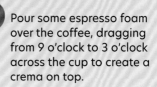

4

Next, draw a treble clef and some musical notes.

5

Use a teaspoon handle or etching tool and some leftover milk to finish the notes on the stave.

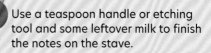

STENCILS

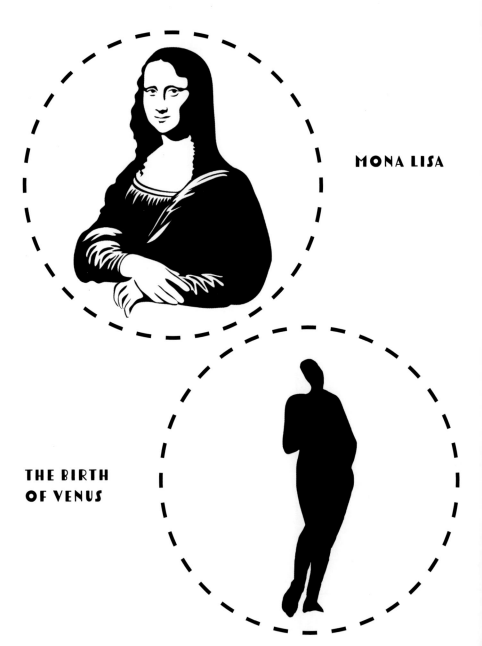

MONA LISA

THE BIRTH
OF VENUS

Trace the stencils below onto a piece of thick card and cut out carefully.

FOOTBALL

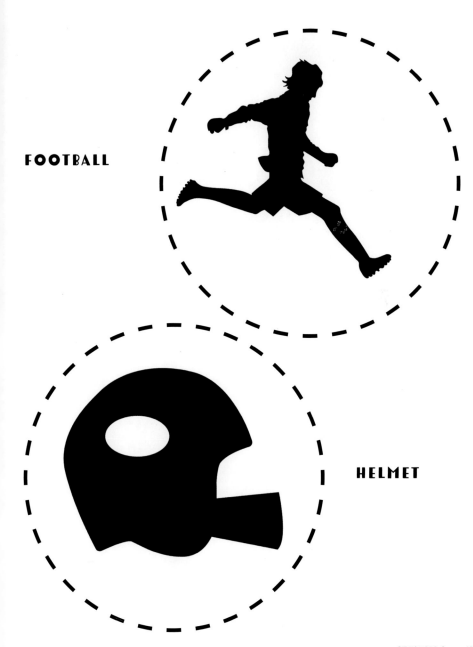

HELMET

YOGA

DIVER

INDEX